Becoming Friends with Chaos

Angel A. James

Becoming Friends with Chaos

Red Giant Books

ISBN: 978-1-7325514-8-0

10 9 8 7 6 5 4 3 2 1

Printed in the United States of America.

www.redgiantbooks.com

All original sketches by Angel James

Photo Credits Angel James, Mitch James, and Erin Spencer

To the memory of my mother.

To my father, for having excellent taste in music.

To my husband, for continuing to love and support me even when I am chasing you around the house saying, "let me read this to you!"

And, of course, to Bob Dylan.

Table of Contents

Foreward

Today Bob Dylan turned eighty, and it is not a coincidence that while I wrote down ideas and had a skeletal sketch for this foreword, I reserved enough time today to bring it to fruition. Things did not go according to the plan. This was the date this book was supposed to be published, along with a concert of Northeast Ohio Musicians covering his songs. A large-scale celebration so that the hometown of The Rock and Roll Hall of Fame could throw a proper birthday party with artists and bands all doing their versions of Dylan songs. Between band changes—a twist—a woman who wrote a book, not a biography, but poems of all different styles and perspectives, would read, engrossing the crowd by showing a relationship with Bob Dylan not totally unlike other mystical relationships, nurtured with faith, passion, imagination, and devotion. Allow me though to rewind to the singularity of this project.

I met Angel at a poetry reading when I found out she had a deep knowledge and appreciation for Ani DiFranco. I mentioned to a few people at the table that, coincidentally, I was one of the editors of *Great Lakes Review,* when Ani had participated in an interview with the itinerant artist Jim Mott. When Angel finished reading and returned to the table, we discussed DiFranco and it was evident she knew much more than I about the subject, but the evening ended in an invitation for another reading hosted by Angel's husband, writer and professor, Mitch James.

I attended that reading and went out to a local bar afterward with the hosts and some of the participants of the reading and had the opportunity to converse with Angel and Mitch. The evening concluded with an impromptu jam session at my house with everyone who played playing (you guessed it) a Bob Dylan song. Something else happened, Angel and Mitch showed great interest in the journal that I had started with a host of other editors from Buffalo, Toronto, Milwaukee and Chicago. This led to knowing for sure that we needed to meet again.

I invited Angel and Mitch to my home to discuss the eventual position of Mitch taking the wheel at *Great Lakes Review*. We had great discussions and I became optimistic about Mitch taking the helm of an enterprise that I had helped to start, and then we started talking about Dylan. And then Angel recited a poem from memory, and I inquired who wrote that? And of course, she was the author. Then she recited another. At this point, the original reason for all of us to get together could wait because there was something happening and all of my energy and focus immediately shifted, I went into my office and grabbed a piece of paper (Full disclosure, there was bourbon present so I may be a bit off on some of the details but I'm confident that I'm accurate enough to catch the spirit of the evening. More on this below.) and asked Angel to sign an almost illegible pledge that went something like "Angel James will deliver the Bob Dylan Poems one year from tonight." She accepted and signed with some hesitation at first which eventually turned into acceptance and determination.

When my new, talented friends left, I thought, I will do what I can to have this book published on May 24th, 2021, Dylan's 80th birthday, and I knew there was already a buzz about having a concert. This was just one of many plans that I had for the coming year, as many no doubt can relate. Angel and Mitch were my last nonfamily, non-socially distanced, non-masked guests who I have had over indoors from that night until now. So, the best laid plans of mice and men and Dylan fans will have to adapt, and the belated birthday is coming, and while of course, few people know much about the elusive, misdirecting Bob Dylan, I think we would both lay our bets that he would not want a random, discretionary date to get in the way of a party, especially one with so much music and poetry to experience.

The reader may notice that Angel and I have a slightly different recollection of the night that led to this book. That's OK. I'm skeptical of memory because it is selective and I believe we have evolved so that the function of memory must not have served our species with the highest utility of being completely accurate. However, no matter which version is more accurate, mine or Angel's, or if history lies somewhere in between , there is one thing that I'm completely certain of: we always did feel the same, we just saw it from a different point of view.

Rob Jackson
May 24th, 2021

Becoming Friends with Chaos

Introduction

When I try to recall my earliest memories of Bob Dylan being a part of my life, one particular cluster of events comes to mind. It begins in my 7th grade English classroom. I am twelve years old. I am holding a copy of *The House of Seven Gables* trying to decide if it would be the next book I read to add to my page count so I could get that amazing Book-It pin that made the best noise when you scratched it and meant the promise of a Pizza Hut personal pan pizza with my mom when I overhear two teachers discussing something involving the lyrics of "Blowin' in the Wind." I am young and have not yet developed the mental discipline not to eaves drop, and I overhear that they are butchering the lyrics and I jump in to save them. I recite the first two verses (why I didn't just say the whole song, I am not sure) and they both stop talking and turn their heads to look at me. One of the teacher's mouths drop open just a wee bit and I am not certain, then nor now, if it was because she was impressed with my incredible Bob-Dylan-song-recitation skills or if she was annoyed that I was eaves dropping and then interrupted their adult conversation to correct them.

Either way, this is where the cluster of memories begins. At twelve years old when I have already committed many Bob Dylan songs to memory. The next part of this memory journey is in this same 7th grade English class when one of our assignments was to memorize and recite poems in front of everyone. Other kids very likely hated this assignment, but I was stoked. I performed "The Jabberwocky." I recall practicing my performance for my dad as we painted the upstairs office of Denny's

Beer Barrel Pub. I had known all the words for years, as *Alice's Adventures in Wonderland & Through the Looking Glass* has been my favorite book for as long as I can remember. After I was done reciting the words, dad popped his head from around a corner where he had been painting and said, "You can't just say the words, you have to feel them. You're telling a story." Then he recited the story of "Alice's Restaurant" by Arlo Guthrie from memory to prove his point (and because he was a showoff). He taught me to love music that told stories. Music and poetry from storytellers like Bob Dylan.

I remember trying desperately to learn all the words to "Subterranean Homesick Blues." I'm nearly there, after all these years. I remember painting with dad and hearing him belt out "I ain't gonna work on Maggie's farm no more!" I remember buying my first beat up guitar from a pawn shop for $100 and learning to play "The Times They Are A'Changing." Dylan has been so infused into my life from such a young age that I can't even dig back far enough into the recesses of my mind to pinpoint the exact moment of introduction.

Dylan's songwriting is so profound and prolific that, according to The Bob Dylan Project, as of January 11, 2020, a whopping 6,000 artists have covered his music. When a Bob Dylan cover song comes on the TV or the radio, one of my favorite games I play with my husband is to make him guess who wrote it. The answer is clearly always the same. (He's catching onto me, finally.) I attempted to write a poem about it, which you'll discover later.

At the risk of serving up such an unpopular opinion so early on in this book, I have to admit I much prefer the Dave Matthews Band cover of "All Along the Watchtower" over any other (sorry, Jimi). And while we're on the topic of cover songs, I would be remiss not to mention a few of my favorites.

The idea of cover songs is interesting to me. Dylan himself has spoken on his preferences towards other artists covering his music; artists who imbue the song with the same feeling and intention Dylan had envisioned the song would have, rather than taking that song out into "left field."[1] There is no way to be certain of Dylan's intentions or what he means by "left field," but the thing I appreciate most about a well-covered song is reimagining the song and injecting it with new life. In essence, for me a well-covered song gives the song a new home. My most favorite cover songs feel like old friends. Sometimes they make me stop and reconsider the meaning of the lyrics in a way I would not have otherwise. They give the words a new mouthfeel. Many other people in the music industry with far more reputable qualifications than myself have compiled lists of the best covers of Dylan's music, so I will keep my list of personal picks abridged. Here are my favorite Dylan covers in alphabetical order:

"A Hard Rain's A-Gonna Fall" – Laura Marling

Marling makes this song feel like a secret she's slowly revealing. The creeping crescendo, the driving rhythm, the smooth harmonies, and her mystical, magical voice. That voice! Marling honors the tradition of the song from *The Freewheelin'*

1 Bob Dylan, *Chronicles : Volume 1*, 61.

Bob Dylan and injects electric energy into the poetry of the piece.

"All Along the Watchtower" – Dave Matthews Band

There are plenty of live versions of this song to gush over, but I am at my happiest when I hear Dave and his bandmates get into the rhythm of this jam for ten minutes or more. I could listen to this song forever. A couple favorites of mine are from the 2019 Central Park concert and the 2011 concert at the Gorge. The improv intro. The slow sultry and haunting creep up into an explosion of sound and lights. The emotion in Dave's voice! The growl! And then the jam. Then the beautiful, fiery, soul-shaking jam. Yes, please.

"Don't Think Twice, it's Alright" – Kesha

Talk about an emotional, gut-wrenching, slap in the face. This is one of my all-time favorite songs as it is, but then for Kesha, in the midst of her own personal and professional turmoil, to pour her pain and heart and soul into this song… it definitely still brings tears to my eyes.

"It Ain't Me Babe" – First Aid Kit

I could listen to these women sing all day. The tonality and harmonies these women create give me chills. I just adore them. They very much honor the original spirit of the song and imbue it with the clarity that comes in hindsight and the longing that comes with lost love.

"Leopard-Skin Pillbox Hat" – Beck

If you don't love this cover, just fuck right off. And that's all I have to say about that.

"Ring Them Bells" – Sarah Jarosz

I adore this song, and I especially adore Dylan's original version. So clean. Jarosz makes this piece soulful and effortless. She brings an innocence to this song that differs from the sage wisdom in Dylan's voice, and her sweet vocals makes it feel more like an invocation than a performance.

"Subterranean Homesick Blues" – The Lumineers

That cello! Oh, the instrumentals on this piece are entrancing. The spirit of the strings in this cover is reminiscent of Scarlet Rivera in "Rolling Thunder Revue;" a haunting melody and so much power in the performance. My favorite things about this cover are that The Lumineers 1. made it minor, 2. managed to strip it back and re-envision it (maybe I feel this way because there is no harmonica?), 3. made it a jam! Seeing this song live is incredible.

This little passion project was born out of a music and alcohol-fueled evening with my husband and Rob, a friend of ours. After jamming on a couple of Bob Dylan tunes, I told Rob I wrote a couple poems about Bob Dylan and asked if he'd like to hear them. Rob obliged. After I'd finished, Rob, in his incredibly kind and alcohol-amplified enthusiasm, declared that I should write a collection of works inspired by Bob Dylan. "Anything you want," he said. He gave me a year to produce a draft.

Now I don't know what year you are in presently with this book in your hands, but let me tell you a little something about the year 2020 (in which I wrote this book—all save but the two poems I shared with Rob that fateful evening). It was a dumpster fire. That is putting it rather gently, as I reflect on the past year while I write the rest of this introduction.

I tried my best to write the "Talkin' 2020 Blues" to evoke the spirit of Dylan's "Talkin' World War III Blues," but after the first 14 verses and copious notes, it honestly became too depressing for me to work on. Maybe I'll get around to finishing it someday. Maybe I'll send my incomplete pile of verses to Todd Snyder. He'd have a ball with it, I like to imagine.

This project was a delightful distraction to pour myself into, and for that I must thank Rob for giving me something productive to work on. Thanks, Rob!

By now, I'm sure that you, dear reader, have gathered that this book is the embodiment of my profound appreciation and deep respect for Bob Dylan. Initially, my admiration stemmed primarily from Dylan's music, but as the years went on, and as I began doing research for this project, my admiration encompassed so much more. I've attempted to cluster my inspirations thematically based on the research that I've done and the works that I've read. Not every poem in this collection utters the name Bob Dylan, but I hope each piece evokes his spirit.

Without further ado...

The Newport Poems

Expectation and Consequence

All the pens are gone
and everyone's looking
around for the words I'm
not writing
and the message I'm
not sending
and the life I'm
not leading.

They turn to one another
with their hands
in the air.
They question
my presence.
They think
I'm Not There

but I couldn't be
any closer if I
touched them.

They all thought I was
dead before I
started dying.
At night with my
eyes closed
I can still hear them
crying.

Arms waving in
the air, I wail
"stop, here I am!"
No one even looks up.
They just pluck out
my mind and lock it
up in a box
and seal it

and stamp it
"1965"

***

Sometime long after
Christ died
somewhere along the
road I walked past him
and Bob Dylan
with their crosses
and cigarettes.

And Christ said, "Hey Bobby,
you had some good shit to
say. I like that one about
Abraham and his son
on the highway."

Through his black
sunglasses and cigarette
smile he said, "Thanks man,
you had a good sound too.
Revolutionary if I remember
correctly. But somewhere it
went sour. You should have
stuck to your early stuff.
It must have been
the electric guitar."

Sea Change (That Prick Now)

Well, it had to get there. It had to go that way for me. Because that's where I started and eventually it just got back to that.

-Bob Dylan[2]

when you've got it all along
when you started there
when you were grinding on the piano
so hard Little Richard style
that the principal pulled
the curtain on you
at the talent show
when it was electric traded
for first acoustic
can anyone really say
that at twenty-three years old
in 1965 there was a
sea change?
that you broke folk?

how quickly one can
turn from hailing you as
Jesus Christ himself
before crying out
Judas Iscariot
the great betrayer
and for what?
like a rolling stone?
how does it feel to be
on your own?

imagine being the one who rebelled
against Dylan's electric
imagine being that prick now

2 Jonathan Cott, *Bob Dylan: The Essential Interviews*, 208.

New Criticism (I)

What is the new criticism?
Give it a close read.
Everything you need
is right in front of you.
Look at the language.
Rhythm and rhyme.
Conflict and context.
Structure and syntax.

Poetry is the language of
revolution.

Tell me something
new. Anything, please.
Apart from the abandonment
of authenticity
or the shirking of responsibility.

There is no intentional
fallacy here.

New Criticism (II)

> *Reporters would shoot questions at me and I would tell them repeatedly that I was not a spokesman for anything or anybody and that I was only a musician. [...] Later an article would hit the streets with the headline "Spokesman Denies That He's a Spokesman." I felt like a piece of meat that someone has thrown to the dogs.*
>
> - Bob Dylan[3]

What is the new criticism?
Speak the words into
being—tell me
what they mean.

What is the new criticism?
Electricity as evolution.
Plugging into the vibrations
on the street. Can you
hear it?

No.

"Spokesman denies that he's a spokesman."
I am not your piece of meat.

What is the new criticism?
It means it takes more than one
instrument to form a band.
More than one voice
to make harmony.

It means it's hard to fight the enemy
without an army.

3 Bob Dylan, *Chronicles: Volume One*, 119.

Evolution is compulsory.
The new criticism
is constant change.

Get on board, motherfucker.
Your folk artist is dead.

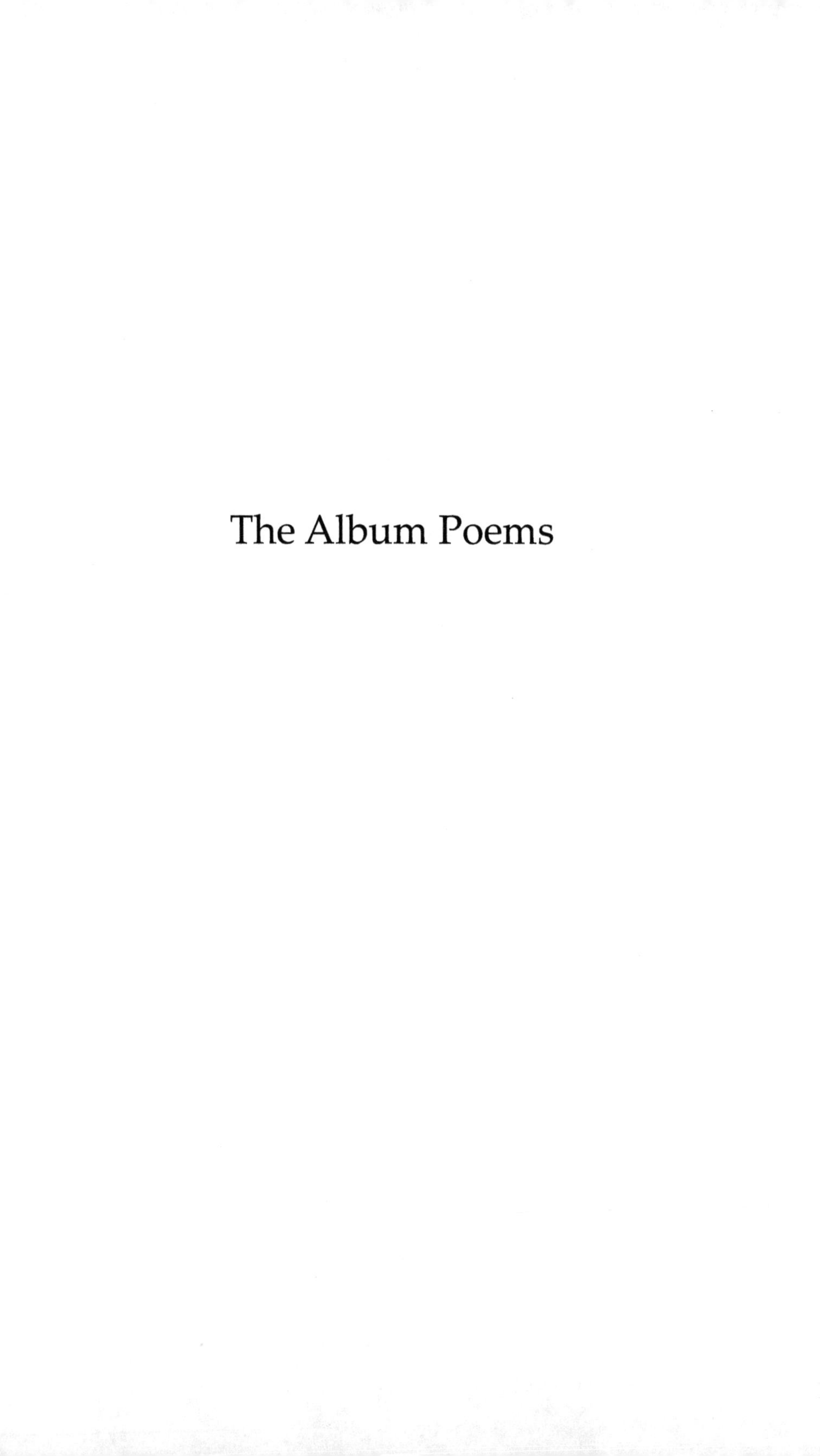

The Album Poems

So Young, So Wise

Bob Dylan, 1962

white boy belting blues
harmonica like freight train
so young, voice so wise

Fingers on the Pulse of Change

The Freewheelin' Bob Dylan, 1963

Every single day I'm
learning something new.
Love and war, babe,
they're giving me the blues.
Got my ear to the ground
and twenty-two years may not
seem like much, but
I've got my fingers on the pulse of change
all the same.

The awakening is hardest when
it happens in a flash.
Flames scorched the veil.
There is no crawling back
into the cave now.
Hard to find trust in the shadows
and Truth's out hanging on the gallows.
Love and war, love and war, babe,
they treat me just the same.

Trying to shake this feeling that I'm
getting left behind
when I'm the one doing the leaving.
I got the highway on my mind.
Second chances are hard to come by
but, babe, I'm going through some changes.
This love ain't worth its weight in pages.
Love and war, love and war, babe,
they treat me just the same.

Revolutionary River[4]

The Times They Are A-Changing, 1964

Resistance is a reactive state of mind. While it can be necessary for survival and to prevent catastrophic harm, it can also tempt us to set our sights too low. [...] Every leap forward for American democracy – from slavery's abolition to women's suffrage to minimum-wage laws to the Civil Rights Act to gay marriage – has been traceable to the revolutionary river, not the resistance. In fact, the whole of American history can be described as a struggle between those who truly embraced the revolutionary idea of freedom, equality and justice for all and those who resisted.

- Michelle Alexander, *We Are Not the Resistance*

On poverty

08 Jan 1964 – "Johnson Declares War On Poverty." *The Central New Jersey Home News*, New Brunswick, NJ

08 May 1964 – "GOP Stages 'Sit-out' On Poverty Bill: House-Unit Democrats in Caucus, Accused of 'Lock-Out.'" *The Baltimore Sun*, Baltimore, MD

11 May 1964 – "The great war on poverty: The United States has the capacity and resources to wage and win the war on poverty." *The Morning News*, Wilmington, DE

06 Dec 1964 – "Economic Opportunity Act Has Historic Possibilities." *Arizona Republic*, Phoenix, AZ

4 The following are all very real headlines pulled from newspapers kept explicitly to the years 1964 and 2020. The headlines pulled are not an exhaustive coverage of the topics, Michelle Alexander, "We Are Not the Resistance ," The New York Times, Sept. 21, 2018.

06 Aug 2020 – "Most Americans don't have enough assets to withstand 3 months without income." *science daily.com*

07 Oct 2020 - "COVID-19 to Add as Many as 150 Million Extreme Poor by 2021." *worldbank.org*

15 Oct 2020 – "Coronavirus: US poverty rises as aid winds down." *BBC.com*

On LGBTQ

20 Jan 1964 – "Youths—And Adults—Woefully Ignorant On Homosexuality." *The Journal Herald*, Dayton, OH

01 Mar 1964 – "Homosexuality is Symptom of Serious Psychological Trouble." *The Post-Crescent*, Appleton, WI

25 Oct 1964 – "Homosexuals: A Puzzle to Scientists." *The Miami Herald*, Miami, FL

06 Jun 2020 – "Supreme Court Delivers Major Victory to LGBTQ Employees." *National Public Radio*

13 Jun 2020 – "Trump administration erases health are protections for transgender patients during Pride Month." *CBS News*

21 Oct 2020 – "Francis becomes 1st pope to endorse same-sex civil unions." *apnews.com*

On voting

24 Jan 1964 – "24th Amendment Ratified: LBJ Hails Poll Tax Defeat." *The Miami News*, Miami, FL

01 Apr 1964 – "Voting Rights Section Defended as 'Modest Step' By Supporters." *Fort Lauderdale News*, Fort Lauderdale, FL

31 Dec 1964 – States Move Toward "One Man, One Vote." *The Kansas City Times*, Kansas City, MO

30 Mar 2020 – "Trump says Republicans would 'never' be elected again if it was easier to vote." *The Guardian*

09 Jun 2020 – "GOP recruits army of poll watchers to fight voter fraud no one can prove exists: Voting rights advocates worry the effort will target and intimidate minority voters." *NBC News*

06 Jul 2020 – "Supreme Court says a state may require presidential electors to support its popular-vote winner." *The Washington Post*

17 Aug 2020 – "In commemorating the 100th anniversary of the 19th Amendment, let's remember the battle for equality is FAR from over. *NBC News*

05 Nov 2020 – "Trump calls for vote counting to stop as path to victory narrows, Biden urges all to 'stay calm.'" *ABC News*

06 Nov 2020 – "Romney: Trump's election fraud claim wrong, 'reckless.'" *apnews.com*

10 Dec 2020 – "Texas joined by 17 red states in Supreme Court lawsuit to overturn Trump's election defeat." *Independent.co.uk*

12 Dec 2020 – "Supreme Court Dismisses Texas Lawsuit Aiming To Overturn Election Results." *NPR*

On race

17 Apr 1964 – "LBJ Deplores Racial Violence: Says All Groups Should Try to Understand Other's Viewpoint." *The Progress*, Clearfield, PA

26 May 1964 – "Complete Text of Civil Rights Bill, H.R. 7152, Now Before U.S. Senate." *Daily Press*, Newport News, VA

02 Jun 1964 – "Rights Walk Is Hailed As Success." *The Fresno Bee The Republican*, Fresno, CA

20 Jun 1964 – "Senate Approves Civil Rights Act: Historic Measure Passes 73-27; Debate Longest in Body's History." *Green Bay Press-Gazette*, Green Bay, WI

23 Jun 1964 – "Three Civil Rights Workers Disappear in Mississippi." *Santa Cruz Sentinel*, Santa Cruz, CA

03 Jul 1964 – "Johnson Signs Rights Act, Legality Will Be Tested." *Portage Daily Register*, Portage, WI

22 Jul 1964 – "Race Riots Of Past Shed Light on Weekend Violence in Harlem: Tensions Caused By Changing Relations Seen As Common Factor In Riots." *The Record*, Hackensack, NH

27 Jul 1964 – "'New Breed' of Demonstrator at Civil Rights Riots." *The Napa Valley Register*, Napa, CA

27 Jul 1964 – "New York Race Riots Are Front-Page News Throughout Europe." *The Post-Star*, Glens Falls, NY

10 Aug 1964 – "White Youth, Negro Die In Two Racial Clashes." *The Boston Globe*, Boston, MA

14 Oct 1964 – "Rev. Dr. King Awarded Nobel Peace Prize." *The Berkshire Eagle*, Pittsfield, MA

05 Dec 1964 – "Mississippi Sheriff, Deputy Among 21 Nabbed by FBI in 3 Civil Rights Murders." *The Morning Call*, Allentown PA

01 Jun 2020 – "Protesters Dispersed With Tear Gas So Trump Could Pose at Church." *The New York Times*

17 Jun 2020 – "6 people of color have died in recent string of hangings across country." *The Atlanta Journal-Constitution*

22 Jun 2020 – "Police say deaths of black people by hanging are suicides. Many black people aren't so sure. (Even the official cause echoes the history of the lynching era)" *The Washington Post*

23 Jun 2020 – "USA: End unlawful police violence against Black Lives Matter protests." *Amnesty International*

24 Jun 2020 – "George Floyd's death was 'murder' and the accused officer 'knew what he was doing,' Minneapolis police chief says." *CNN News*

25 Jun 2020 – "House approves police reform bill named in honor of George Floyd." *CNN News*

25 Jun 2020 – "Impatience grows for cops' arrests in Breonna Taylor's death." *AP News*

29 Jun 2020 – "Cops in Riot Gear Stormed a Violin Vigil for Elijah McClain." *The Cut*

On citizenship

19 May 1964 –"Court Says Naturalized Citizen Can Not Lose

Citizenship For Merely Living Abroad." *The Times and Democrat*, Orangeburg, SC

18 Jun 2020 – Supreme Court blocks Trump from ending DACA in big win for Dreamers." *NBC News*

On war and foreign relations

22 May 1964 – "Fear of Red China Growing." *The Oneonta Star*, Oneonta, NY

24 May 1964 – "Red China Viewed as Biggest Enemy." *The Times*, Shreveport, LA

21 Jun 1964 – "U.S. Must Stay or Cease to Be Pacific Power." *The Los Angeles Times*, Los Angeles, CA

06 Aug 1964 –"Viet Attack 'Highly Successful'… McNamara: Attacks To Be Blasted, U.S. Tells UN Council." *The Cincinnati Enquirer*, Cincinnati, OH

30 Sept 2020 – "The U.S. and China could slip into a 'new cold war' that pushes countries to pick sides." *CNBC.com*

19 Oct 2020 – "Sleepwalking Into World War III: Trump's Dangerous Militarization of Foreign Policy." *foreignaffairs.com*

09 Nov 2020 – "The End of 'America First': How Biden Says He Will Re-engage with the World." *The New York Times*

On environmental protections

07 Aug 1964 – "Congress Expected To Act Soon On Approval For Wilderness Act." *The Selma Times-Journal*, Selma, AL

01 Jan 2020 – "Trump Removes Pollution Controls on Streams and Wetlands." *The New York Times*, New York, NY

06 Feb 2020 – "Trump team finalizes plans for drilling, mining in shrunken Utah national monuments." *The Los Angeles Times*, Los Angeles, CA

10 Mar 2020 –"Trump Move to Gut NEPA, Bedrock U.S. Environmental Law, Would SlashProtection for Air, Water, Wildlife." *Center for Biological Diversity*

06 Jul 2020 – Dakota Access Pipeline Must Shut own, Judge Rules." *The Wall Street Journal*

06 Jul 2020 – Developers Abandon the Atlantic Coast Pipeline for Good." *Natural Resources Defense Council*

06 Nov 2020 –"Biden Reaffirms Commitment to Rejoining Paris Agreement." *EcoWatch*

On women's rights

18 Sept 1964 –"Suffragettes of 1920s Still Busy in Fight for Equal Rights for Women." *The South Bend Tribune*, South Bend, IN

26 Sep 1964 – "Suffragette Still Fights for Rights." Standard-Speaker, Hazelton, PA

12 Mar 2020 –"Weinstein Rape Sentence in US Boosts #MeToo Movement: New Treaty Will Help Protect Women in the Workplace." *Human Rights Watch*

29 Jun 2020 – "Supreme Court strikes down restrictive Louisiana abortion law that would have closed clinics." *The Washington Post*

08 Jul 2020 – "Supreme Court upholds Trump's rollback of birth control coverage mandate." *Politico.com*

On Bob Dylan

16 Feb 1964 - "Explosive, Haunting Style Of Troubadour Bob Dylan: Folk Singer Bob Dylan Recording an Album in New Your City." *The San Francisco Examiner,* San Francisco, CA

15 Jun 2020 - "Bob Dylan Has Given Us One of His Most Timely Albums Ever With 'Rough and Rowdy Ways.'" *Rolling Stone.com*

29 Jun 2020 – "Bob Dylan Is Still the Voice of a Generation." *Vulture.com*

Get Born

Bringing it All Back Home, 1965

the kids would
call it
"woke"
these days
but the sentiment
is the same

Single Train of Thought

Slow Train Coming, 1979

If I were a single train of thought,
I'd be long gone into the sunset
left with miles and miles of tracks headed
to nowhere.
I'd follow the sun west. Off into that sun
set. That's right. I'd follow you,
motherfucker.
Wait, what was I talking about?
Oh yeah...that single train of thought.
It's long gone.

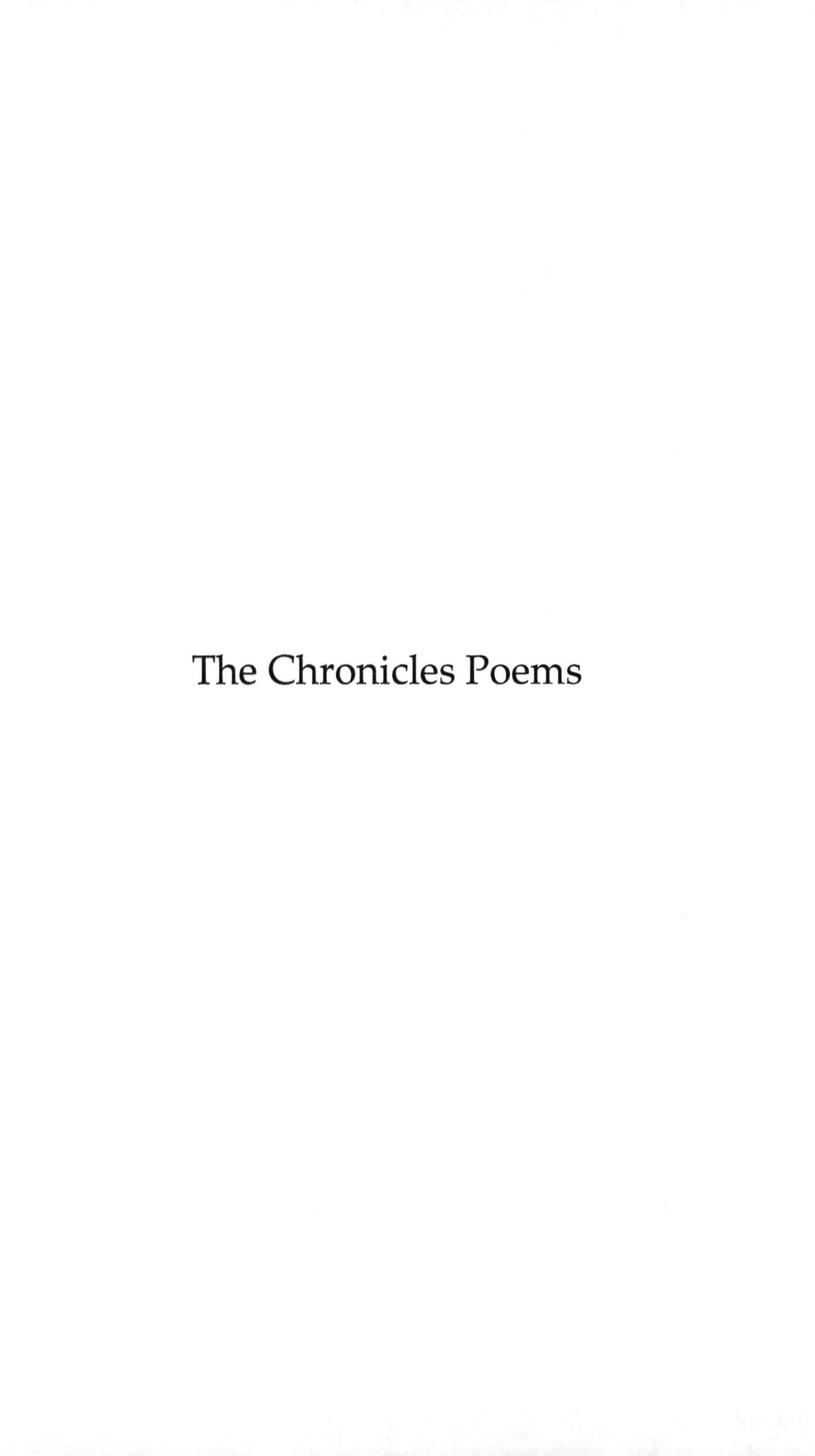

The Chronicles Poems

What Kind of Poet

MacLeish tells me that he considers me a serious poet and that my work would be a touchstone for generations after me, that I was a postwar Iron Age poet but that I had seemingly inherited something metaphysical from a bygone era.

- Bob Dylan [5]

Serious and subtle
black leather and shoestrings
touchstone of a generation
postwar posthaste
Iron Age rust belt
poet of poems that are
actually songs.

Heartland
West Coast
East Coast
North Country
Appalachian Mountain
Jug band stomp and holler songs.

At the kitchen counter
with a pot of coffee
metaphysical and cerebral
mythic and mysterious
can't even relate to the generation
trying to lead a quiet kind of life poet.

Pounding the midnight streets
passing the basket
climbing up the fire escape
hopping on the D train
don't know how to do much else poet.

5 Bob Dylan, *Chronicles: Volume One*, 111.

I Wish I Were Water

Some days when I am a
vast mountain,
stunning expanse,
perilous,
I wish I were sky.
Lighter – easier to breath.
And on days when I am sky,
roiling clouds looming,
dark and foreboding,
I wish I were water.
Serene and in constant motion.
There is no satisfying the wanderer,
and no one can step inside the same
me twice.

Sometimes when I am grounded,
my feet become tree roots
digging deep into the dirt
in search of other tree roots
to entangle with so we can whisper
to one another, "oh, don't you wish
we were birds?"

And sometimes in flight I stretch
out my wings so wide I get
caught in the updraft
sending me sailing
and when I am safely
clasping branches between
my toes I whisper, "oh,
how I wish I were
tethered to the earth."
There is no satisfying the wanderer
but, oh, how I wish I were water.
Serene and in constant motion.

Missing Person

There was a missing person inside of myself and I needed to find him.

- Bob Dylan[6]

Excuse me, have you
seen this girl?
Her eyes are
blue sometimes.
In the confounding way
that water is blue.
A refraction of whatever is
nearby. No color of its own.
Character by proxy.

There is a missing
person inside myself
and I need to find her.
I swear I only looked away
for a moment and she was gone.
Slipped off into the recesses.
Fell down a rabbit hole.
Hopped a train headed west.
Jumped a boat seeking warmer shores.
What would she do?
Where would she go?
I am not sure, but
there is a missing person
inside myself
and I need to find her.

What is the difference
between she and me?
Between I and her?

6 Bob Dylan, *Chronicles: Volume One*, 147.

One of them genuine?
One, a performer?
What could it be she's
searching for?

And where does one go
searching for oneself?

I am done for.
An empty burned-out wreck.
I am the shell of the girl
gone searching
for love
for you
for knowledge
for truth
for desire
a distraction
a purpose
persistence, courage
assurance, completion.

And how many of these
things are even real?
I am not sure, but
I will search for her
searching for self
to the ends of the earth.
There is a missing person
inside myself
and I need to find her.

Controlled Burn

In a few years' time a shit storm would be unleahsed.
Things would begin to burn. Bras, draft cards, American flags,
bridges, too—everyone would be dreaming of getting it on.

- Bob Dylan[7]

On the first day, a woman in Cleveland burned
all her bras. Not just her bras, but her
shapewear too. She pushed out her rusted metal
wheelbarrow, made a pile of her undergarments,
the things meant to hold her in, hold her up,
smooth her out. Things with too many
wires and ties and straps. Things that made it difficult to
breathe. She poured gasoline over them and tossed in the
match.

It was not news.
Yet.

But the next day she noticed other women on the
street with waste cans blazing. Someone called the
fire department, but there is little they can do about a
controlled burn. "Don't leave it unattended," they said.
Then the news crew came.
"Women in Cleveland burn their bras and Spanx.
More at 6:00."
The next day, Columbus was on the news.
Then Pittsburgh. Toledo. Detroit.
Controlled burns dotted city streets and country sides like
fireflies. Women everywhere standing in their yards.
Gathered in allies and on street corners
tossing things into the flames.

The men watched with curiosity. Watched
their wives and sisters and mothers and daughters
hovering over pyres like cookpots waiting
with anticipation to see what delicious destruction

7 Bob Dylan, *Chronicles: Volume One*, 292.

comes from a concoction of melting
cosmetic cases and corset bone.
Then the men wondered what they could burn.

Some carried out arm loads of neck ties.
Three-piece suits. Stiff and uncomfortable pointed
patten leather shoes. Some men burned their
football pads. Their affliction shirts.
A Florida man set his father on fire
in the name of dismantling toxic masculinity.
"What's happening to American identity?"
It was printed in the *New York Times, The Washington Post,*
CNN, ABC, NBC, Fox News.
"What's happening to the American identity?"

To our identities.

Next people began burning flags and firearms.
Fires hot enough to melt metal.
They burned Bibles and birth certificates,
social security cards and passports,
marriage certificates and divorce decrees.
Any piece of paper signifying
"who a person is."
Where they are going or where they've been.
Anything signifying who a person "should be"
as a proclamation by anyone in a position of
"authority."

Pyres climbed higher as the flames
licked at incinerating
insecurities, parching the patriarchy,
dismantling the damage of
judgment and hypocrisy.
And slowly, slowly, slowly
these embers turned to ash.
From this ash, we will rise.

Folk Religion

With folk songs embedded in my mind like a religion, it wouldn't matter.
Folk songs transcended the immediate culture.

- Bob Dylan [8]

Enlightenment is an altered state –
a metamorphosis of being.

Some prefer the caterpillar – some
the butterfly.

Pray to the songs of the mountain
become water
take all forms.

Pray to the songs of the valley
become air
rise above.

Pray with every stringed instrument
become sound
reverberate.

8 Bob Dylan, *Chronicles: Volume One*, 27.

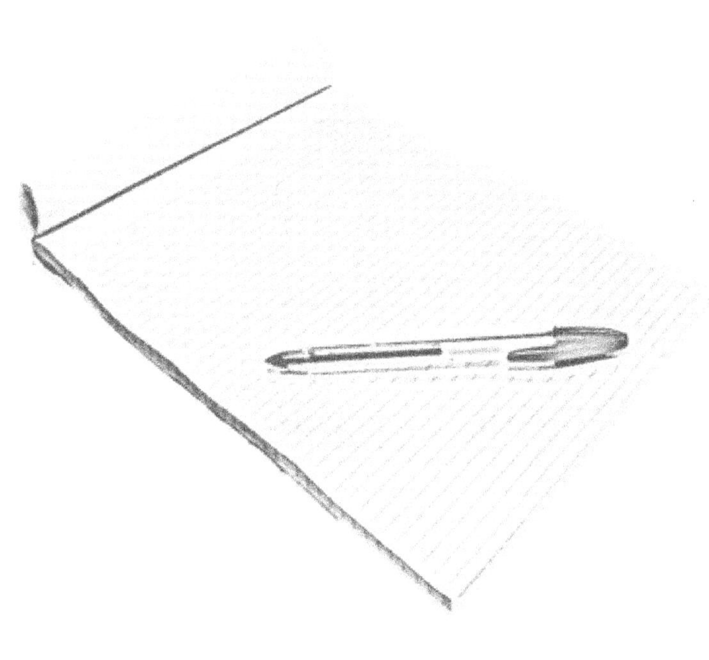

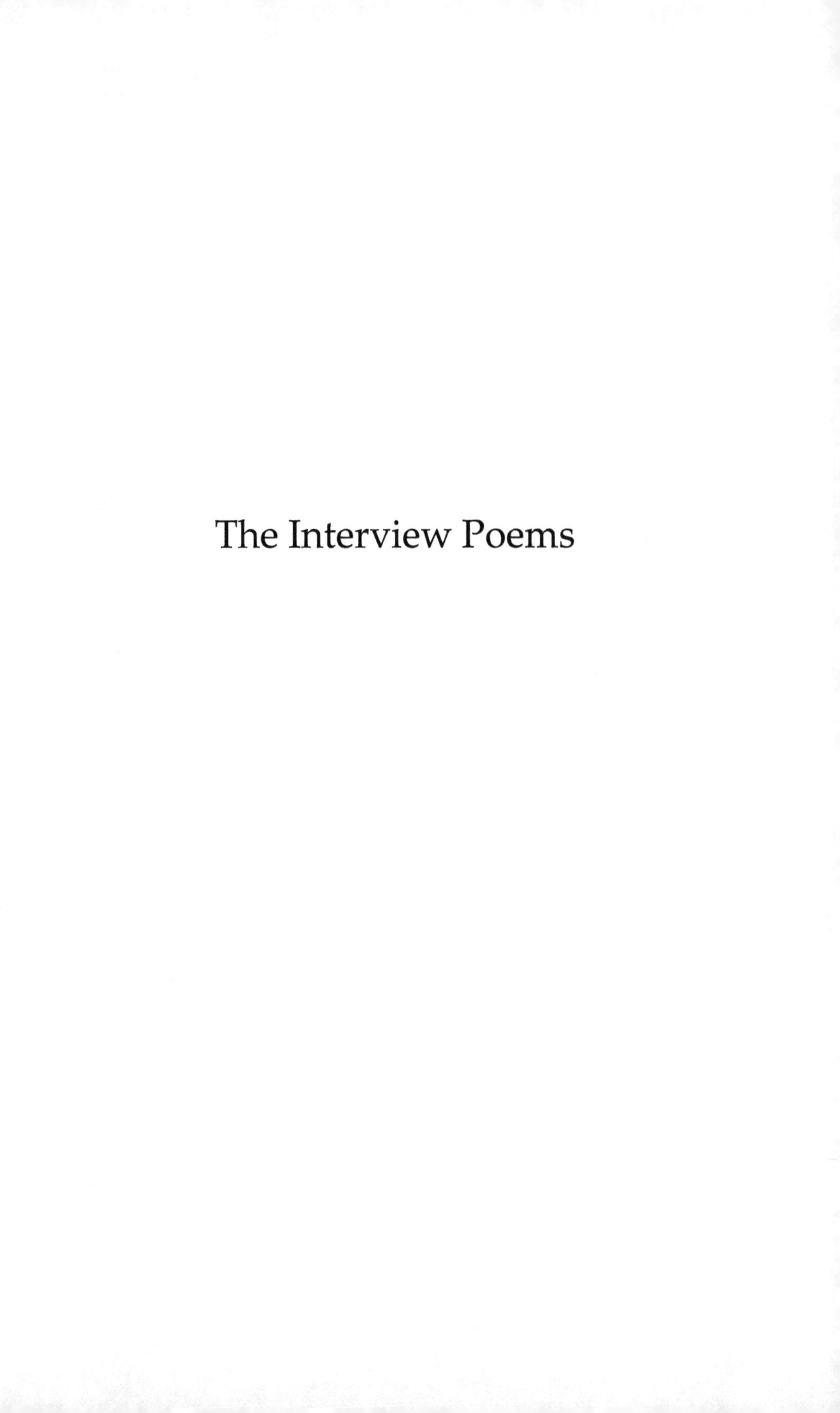

The Interview Poems

Interview

Never give too much
of yourself away
to people who
think they already
own you.

The Act of Naming

Names are labels so we can refer to one another.
But deep inside us we don't have a name. We have no name.

- Bob Dylan [9]

Over this, you have no
control. The distinction
between
the ways that I
am and the things
that I do.

A name is a tiny
box with a locked lid.
An eggshell to puncture,
fracture, step outside of.

To break free from.

A label is what you
peel off a bottle
slick with sweat from
summer heat,
pill between your fingers
and discard.

9 Jonathan Cott, *Bob Dylan: The Essential Interviews*, 206.

Boat Builder

I don't particularly think that God wants me thinking about Him all the time. I think that would be a tremendous burden on Him, you know. He's got enough people asking Him for favors. He's got enough people asking Him to pull strings. I'll pull my own strings, you know.

- Bob Dylan[10]

a lifeline is made from
hands that fell trees
rough cut lumber hewn smooth
hands that know the heft of
holding tools
the weight of hauling their own
burdens up a mountain face
then carrying them
down again
the satisfaction of chiseling
the trunk of an oak into an ark

Christ was a carpenter, after all.

10 Jonathan Cott, *Bob Dylan: The Essential Interviews,* 234.

Becoming Friends with Chaos

Chaos is a friend of mine.

- Bob Dylan [11]

First, came Chaos
in all her mystery and majesty.
Her vast expanse. Onyx eyes
gaze into mine and for a moment
I get a glimpse of the abyss.

For me, she is all there is.
My hand in hers cradles the universe.
She gives me night and day,
earth and sky, swelling tides,
darkness and light.

Chaos both creates and fills
the void inside of me.
I press my mouth to hers;
she shows me things I could not see.
She, the secret puller of the string.

Who knows beauty in a fallen
tree, and, underneath, the pain
of a cracked open, sprouting seed.
The destruction of a chrysalis
to bear a beating wing.

We are more than lovers, we are,
too, becoming friends.
She and I—intertwined and timeless.
Forever outwardly expanding.
Together, we are slouching toward entropy.

---

11 Jonathan Cott, *Bob Dylan: The Essential Interviews*, 50.

Survival

It's just a way of survival, you know, it's just what you do, you know.

- Bob Dylan[12]

wake to bird song
first morning light
dig toes in dirt
take a deep breath
connect to the earth
her pulse is your pulse
gather twigs
light fire
boil water

plant seeds
watch things grow
turn soil and toil
learn to build
build a house
a home – a life
yourself

pick up a pen
write words
sing praise in prose
scribe verse

strum a guitar
a banjo, a mandolin
pluck a bass
strike a drum
feel the rhythm

this is survival
tell your tale
growth in all forms
is a love song to the universe

12 Jonathan Cott, *Bob Dylan: The Essential Interviews*, 323.

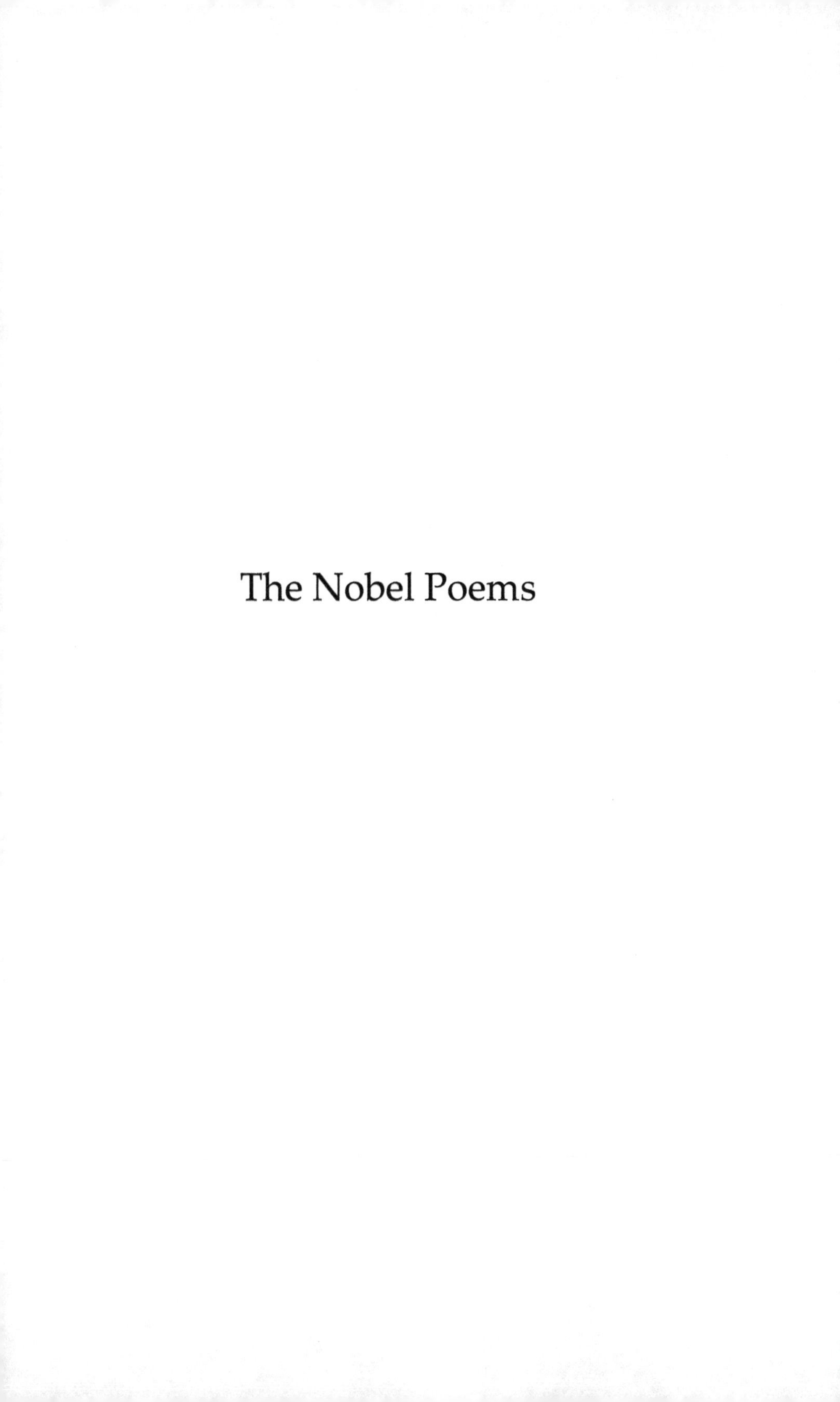

The Nobel Poems

What You Can Get From This is Poetry

Every syllable, every utterance
that pours from your mouth,
your mind, from fingertips to pen
is poetry.
You cannot help yourself.
There is no other way.

Page 3
my life
an explosion
darkness illuminated
I'd never heard of
the New Lost City
but
I wanted to know all about it
I couldn't wait
to learn this music
3

Page 13

Warefare has no limits.

yours is bleeding

corpse.

you'll spend the rest of your life

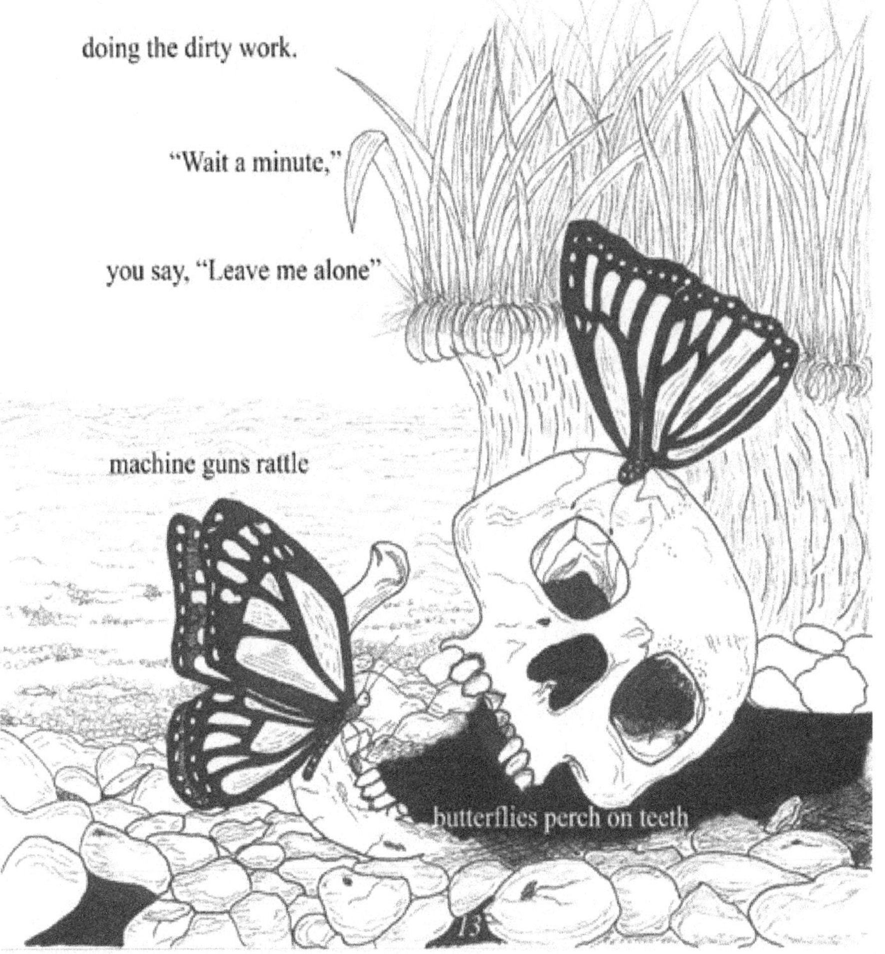

doing the dirty work.
"Wait a minute,"
you say, "Leave me alone"
machine guns rattle
butterflies perch on teeth
13

Page 19

cursed to wander
There's troublemakers
Treachery.
always trying to rescue somebody
There's two roads
to take, and they're both bad.
19

Meant to be Sung

Our songs are alive in the land of the living.
But songs are unlike literature.
They're meant to be sung, not read.

-Bob Dylan[13]

I.
some days pass like
sitting with a dead man
silent and heavy
nowhere to go
effort for naught
Band-Aid on a
broken bone
not safe to stay
not safe to
wander off alone

II.
but other days pass like
wandering with no
direction home
footstep after footstep
traveling slow
ten-year journey
no one knows you
when you get there
no one notices
when you go

III.
all the other days
float—lost at sea
chasing a dream

13 Bob Dylan, *The Nobel Lecture*, 23

IV.
and the point is
songs are meant to be
sung—do you
get it? words on
the page are just that
flat
without the music
the melody
listen

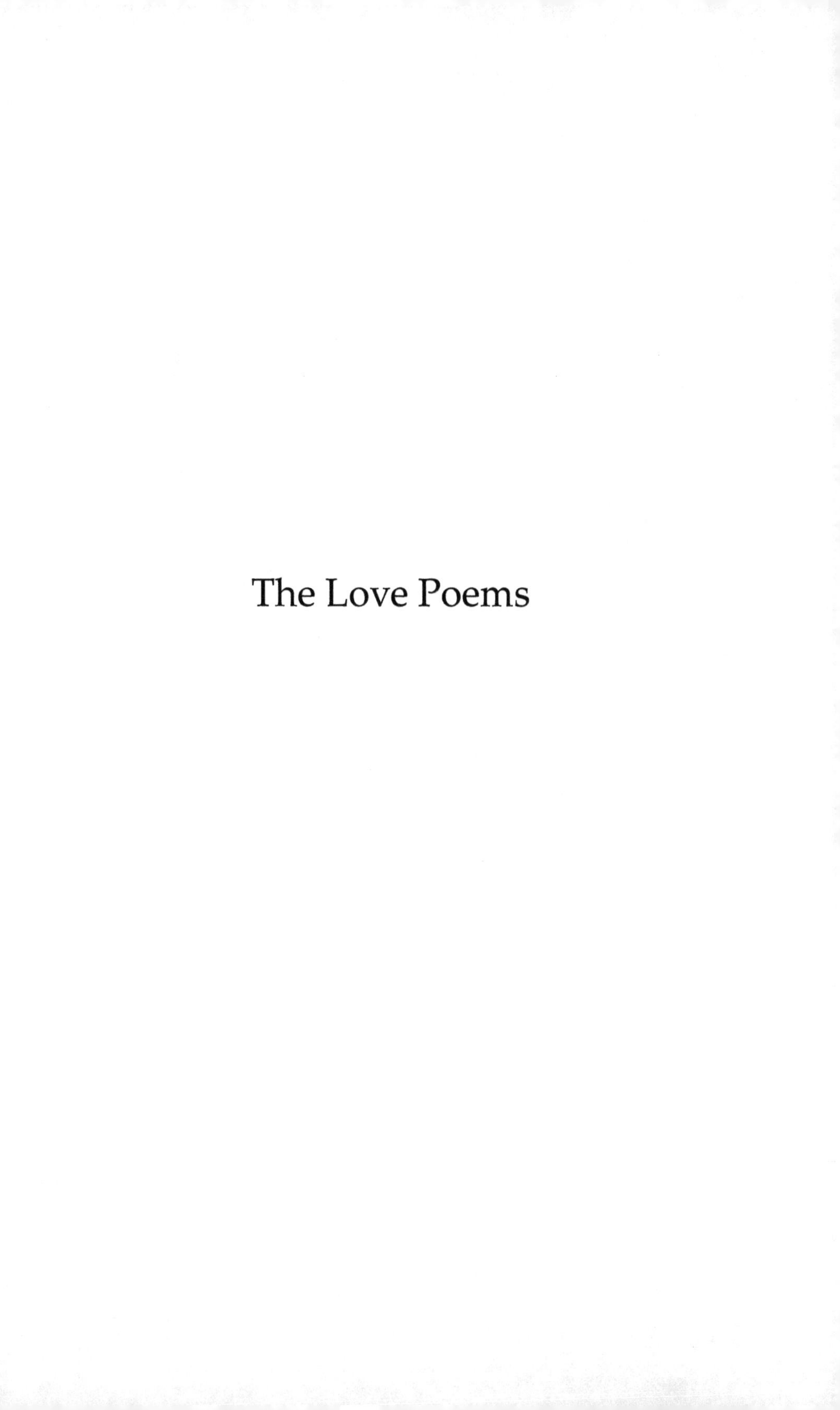

The Love Poems

A Love Letter to Bob Dylan – Nearing His 76th Birthday

As I look at aged black and whites -
artistically faded sepias -
of your untamed curls, cheek bones, chiseled
jaw, boots, hats,
guitars, cigarettes
clinging loosely to your
lower lip,
I am thankful I did not know you
at twenty-six when you were also
twenty-six.
I would have loved you
wholeheartedly—foolishly.
I would have forgotten
my own name.

I might have met you at some late night
party in Greenwich Village. Casually, maybe
I'd have bummed a drag. Maybe mentioned
that I thought "Freewheelin" was just groovy.
That I flipped for "The Times They are A'Changing."
That I'd love to see another side of Bob Dylan.

Then I'd have blushed and winked and wanted to kill myself
all at once.

I'd have looked for you in cafes.
I'd have left you notes that read,

"Why didn't you call?"

and

"I waited for you."

and

"When can I see you again?"

I would have wondered if it was because
I don't smile like Suze
or croon like Joan.

Instead, I love you now.
When you are turning 76
and I am turning 32
which is the age you were when
you released your
15th album.
And I will never meet you, but
I saw you
in concert
and heard you
sing like a
rolling stone.

How does it feel?
How does it feel?

And all I have to tell you now
is you're gonna make me
lonesome when you go.

A Love Letter to Bob Dylan – Nearing His 79th Birthday

What even is the concept of time?
An abstraction?
A line?
You got a fast mind.
I like that.

We're always changing,
me and you.
Our names and faces.
The places we are going to.

All relative to yearning,
it's been a long time coming.
I want you, honey,
I've been waiting.
I can measure the moments.
Feel the hours pass over me.
You got a slick way of talking.
I like that.

A promise is a prayer to time.
Please—still be here tomorrow.
Telling you years ago that I will
love you for years to come.
But only what exists is here
in this multitude of moments
we measure in seconds
in the distance between heartbreak and healing
in the movement of celestial bodies
some circling of the stars
in the color of your eyes against
the light of today's sky.

The moving image of eternity
cannot exist without change.
And we are always changing,
me and you.

We are long gone.
We are not yet.
An abstraction. A line.
In time, on time, out of time, racing against
an absolute.
It's all relative, absolutely, my darlin.

But I promise
I love you now.
I love you now.
I love you now.

A Love Letter to Bob Dylan – Nearing His 80th Birthday

If I'm here at eighty, I'll be doing the same thing.
This is all I want to do. It's all I can do.

- Bob Dylan [14]

You made it, my darling.
You're here.
What would I have ever
done without you?
What else would you have
ever done?

It started with a low hum
a thrumming in the streets
just a beat in your
pocket, a guitar strapped
to your back, boots
on your feet and
no reason to sleep.

Then came fiery frenzy.
Electricity. Mystery.
And I knew the sun
would never set
on you. The light,
my love, you bring
the light.

But, darling,
darkness lives inside
you, too. You paint with
every single shade
of blue.

14 Jonathan Cott, *Bob Dylan: The Essential Interviews*, 346.

In the quiet of my
night, you are the
slow dance.
I can feel my hand
on your chest
hear your heart
beat in my head.

Eventually the frenzy
of a pounding rhythm
becomes a gentle serenade.
It's just the way
things pass by.
If I'm here at eighty
I'll be thinking of you
fondly then too.

Who the Woman Was

Asked who the woman was who broke his heart in song after song,
he laughs and asks, 'Which one? Which song?'

- Bob Dylan[15]

Ours is a safe love.
One where neither you
nor I will ever be
disappointed.

You will love that
I am a guarded lover.
One who slips dollars into
your pocket but never darkens
your doorstep.

And I will love that you
sing my name in
songs sometimes
even if only the
religious ones.

Love like pressing
the headphones so
tightly against my
ears to get you inside
my head.

It would be nice to hear a
different voice in there from
time to time. One that says,
"Is that really important?
Is that really what matters most?"

15 Jonathan Cott, *Bob Dylan: The Essential Interviews*, 391.

We'd never discuss the people
who broke our hearts.
Only what the garden will look like
come springtime and which
books we're going to read next.

I'll never ask
what your songs are about
because, really, I think everyone knows,
but is that really what's important?
Is that really what matters most?

The Poems About Everything Else

I Loved Him First

You nearly took him from me.
In smoke filled bars.
In English classrooms.
In NOLA, on cobblestone streets,
walking around with hurricanes
in our hands.
And all that jazz.

Too many alcohol-fueled nights
I'm pretty sure I regret.
I haven't figured that one out just yet
but you said we couldn't do this anymore.
We couldn't "accidentally" meet up
on Saturday nights at the Saloon
and then you'd take me home with you.

For one of your birthdays I bought you
The Bootleg Series Volumes 1-3 on CD
and I burned them for myself
before handing them over.
I loved him first, after all.

For a long time after we dissipated
into our separate lives it still hurt
to hear him. It made me think of you
and I did not want it to. I did not want it to at all.
I told you once "Desolation Row" reminded me of you.
And you said, "Thanks, I think?"
What I meant then was remember all those nights at Uncle Al's?
The music on the jute box that turned into music of our own.
Fingers pressing six strings that turned into figures lifting the
hem of a shirt. What I mean now is you are so far gone.

The act of bumming a cigarette will always feel
reminiscent of reciting poetry.
After so many years passed, I decided
you cannot take him from me.

I loved him first and love him still
and you are between the windows of the sea—
see through and impossible to grab onto.

Hindsight is the Sharpened Blade

Somewhere between the ages of seven and nine
I broke up a once-lit, barely-hit cigarette into
tiny pieces in the fold-out ashtray of your truck.
Tobacco exposed like freshly tilled dirt.
I did because I knew you shouldn't.
Ignoring the tone in your voice
staring out the breathy fogged up window
knowing I'd surely do it again.

Somewhere between the ages of nine and ten,
in the dark of a basement, I dug
through the remnants of an over-filled ashtray
for the most promising butts and lit them all
taking the final drags from each one.
I don't remember coughing or inhaling.
I'm not certain either took place.
Though I distinctly remember disliking the taste
but doing it anyway.
Because I knew you did it anyway.

I'd lay on the day bed in that darkened basement
and listen to Dylan or the Doors or watch
Dick Van Dyke on the black and white
while you sketched away at I don't know what
but I picked up one of those notebooks once
and landed on a page that read: "It's alright, ma
(I'm only bleeding)."
When I read those words aloud, your
head snapped round, eyes like saucers
until you realized they were your words.
Though I learned that they weren't.

Somewhere between the ages of 30 and 35
I realized they were your words.
I see now that you felt them too,
but the difference between Dylan and you
is when he felt out of time—out of place—

limited by the space he was in
he left
to find what came next.
Did not let his context define his existence.

All this time I always thought
you stayed when you should have left.
Left when you should have stayed.

And hindsight is the sharpened blade
that peels away the years like
layers of dead skin until you get to
the tender flesh of it all
and learn that time does not
heal all things nicely.
Sometimes scar tissue is all that's left.

And the difference between you and me
is I love the leaving.
Knowing the hours of sleep I will accumulate
in that place I used to call home
will never again tally the time it takes me to
drive there.
It's okay to let go of things that
no longer serve you.
It's okay to say goodbye
and mean it.

Reasons for the Whiskey to Have Gone Out of the Bottle[16]

I have not yet read a treatise on
love that teaches you to save
you from yourself.

Moth to the flame.
All aglow but singed
to the bone.
Fruit fly in the glass
of wine. Happily drunk
but drowning.

A vibration so strong
you cannot help but be
shaken toward the
destruction.

Once, you said you wished
you were Dylan, and now
here we are. I'm writing poems
about you. Although I can't imagine
this is what you had in mind.

I can assure you it isn't
what I had in mine.

But, God, you were electric
in the way that I'd let you
burn down my house.
Exposed wiring sparking.

After all this time
I can still feel your hand
on mine, and sometimes I
drink to remember that feeling

---

16 Bob Dylan, *Chronicles: Volume One*, 146

and sometimes I drink to forget
that you're so far away, but
the whiskey's all gone
out of the bottle now.

Sometimes loving
yourself looks like letting go,
no matter the tether
that ties us.

And we are bound, of that
I am certain, but for
what, I do not know.

That Voice is a Memory

you are young and
I am younger still
porcelain figurines sitting
on the windowsill

can't yet understand the
weight of the changing
of the times, but I will

like you, I never
stop moving

stale beer and lingering
cigarette smoke circling
bar lights and distant
eyes that do not reveal
a single secret but I still
want to stand under the
lamplight and keep looking

how old do you need to be
to stop seeking
approval? Your rebellious
heart is a torch
shining a light in the
darkened corners
and I won't pretend to know
you. I am 22 and trying
my very best to relate
to demonstrate that I am
worthy of your attention
of your affection
believing we both have the
best of intentions

turns out leaving is my
most creative invention

I'm gone

but oh that voice is a memory
transporting me instantly
to all these things I've
left behind, tucked them
into the recesses of my mind
that voice pulls me right
outside of time
brings you back to me
like a conjuring
draws you out of the
sound of epiphany
oh that voice of yours
is a memory
take me back

Cover Songs

We play this game
he and I
with a coy smile
I ask him,
Who wrote this song?
Jimi Hendrix, he guessed.
No, babe. It's Bob Dylan.

These are games often played
more than once.
Garth Brooks or the Byrds
Dave Matthews or Adele
and I'd giggle
who wrote the song, not
who's singing it now.
Bob Dylan—it's always Bob Dylan.

Now he jokes with me
Kesha, he teased, or Beck,
The Band, Black Crows, Black Keys,
you tell me
who wrote this song?
Bob Dylan, of course, it's Bob Dylan.

The Park Bench Shoot

If Joan's looks could kill,
Bobby, you'd be dead by now.
Absolutely stone-cold fucking dead.

She forgives you though.
I can see it in the next frame.
Eyes softened, smile somewhat sincere,
Saying… "Damn it, Bobby, why
do you have to be this way?"

Her face in this frame is the embodiment
of the way you love someone and
want to strangle them
at the same time.

Love is death.
Love is slowly dying.

And in the next frame she's
laughing. Open mouthed
eyes crinkled at the corners.

And you still haven't looked at
her, yet. Why?
What are you looking at, Bob?
What do you see?

Let me tell you a thing though.
Let me give you some advice.
When you see Joan for the first time,
and it's been a while, you know,
since you've been on the road together,
and you've been missing her,
and there's some shit between you
that's been left unsaid,
do not ask her what the fuck she's done
to her hair.

Bob and Alice Sit Down to Tea

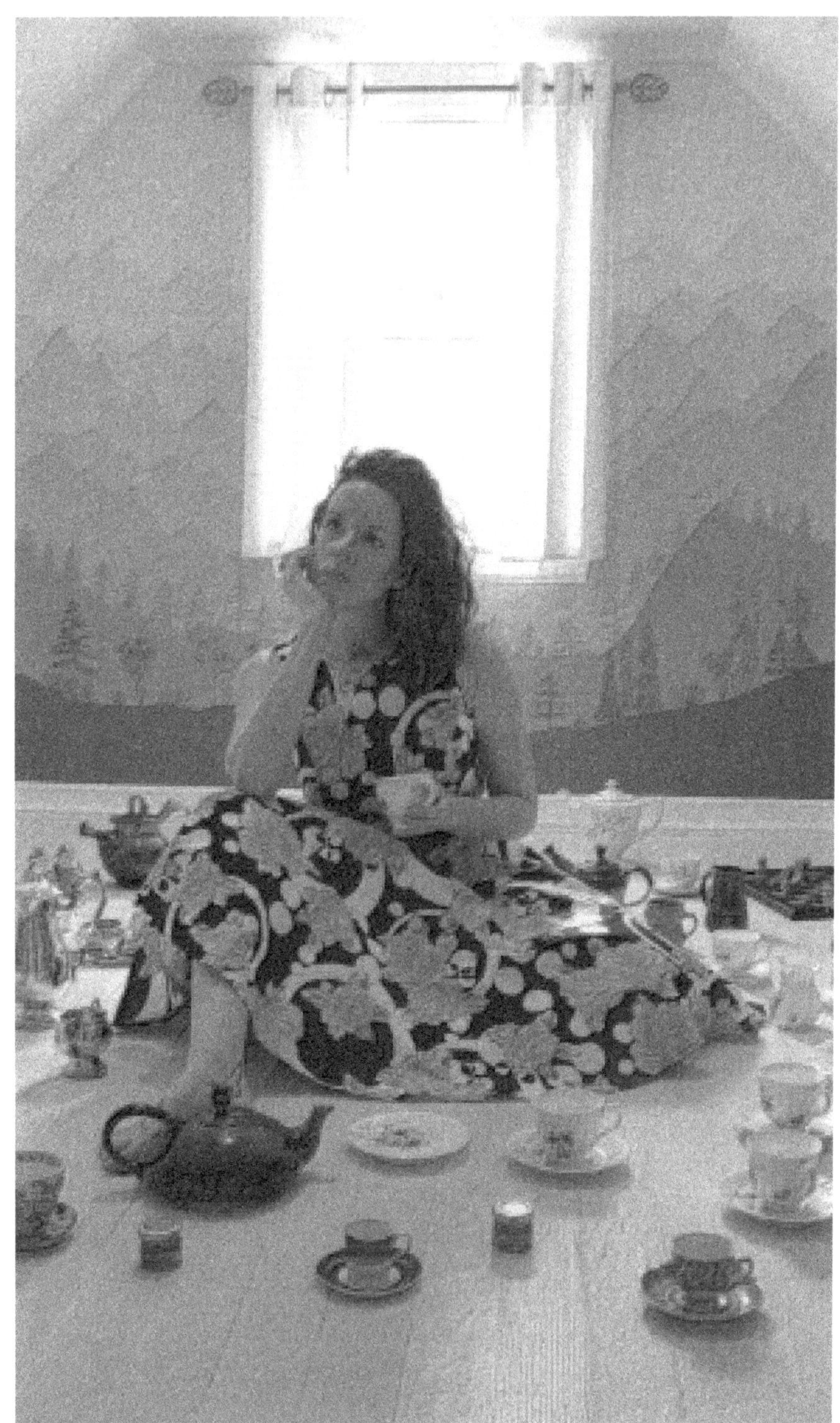

A man walks down a wooded path. The sun sits somewhere above the canopy. It is early afternoon. Birds call to one another. The wind rustles through the trees. He approaches a clearing and comes upon a long table set up for tea. A young girl is seated near the head of the table with her head resting in her hand. She is alone.

Alice: Are you here for tea, then?

Bob: I don't think so. Does anyone know why they are anywhere?

Alice: Well then what have you come for?

Bob: I haven't come for anything. I was just out for a walk.

Alice: Were you looking for something?

Bob: Aren't we all looking for something?

Alice, being a very curious girl herself, is quite pleased to have met someone else who enjoys asking questions. She thinks carefully for a moment before responding, folding her hands in her lap to keep from twiddling her fingers, as the Red Queen instructed.

Alice: Yes, I suppose we are.

Bob: Who are you?

Alice: I—I hardly know, Sir, just at present—at least I know who I *was* when I got up this morning, but I think I must have been changed several times since then. [17]

17 Lewis Carroll, *Alice's Adventures in Wonderland & Through the Looking-Glass*, 49.

Bob: Well, you always know who you are. You just don't know who you're gonna become. [18]

Alice: Well who am I then? Tell me that first, and if I like being that person, we can move on; if not, I'll stay here till I'm someone else. [19]

Bob: Well, I can't answer that, can I? Since we've only just met. Do you know who you are becoming?

Alice: No, but I think I was changed when I got up this morning.

Bob: I think we all wake up changed every morning.

Bob reaches into his pocket and pulls out a small jar of white face paint. He removes the lid and begins to smear the paint onto his face with his fingers.

Alice: Well who are you?

Bob: *Still applying the paint, he says,* I change during the course of a day. I wake and I'm one person, and when I go to sleep I know for certain I'm somebody else. I don't know *who* I am most of the time. It doesn't even matter to me.[20]

Bob finishes applying the face paint, screws the lid back onto the container, places the container back into his pocket, reaches into his bag and pulls out a Stetson hat covered in fresh flowers and places it on his head.

---

18 Sam Shepard, "A Short Life of Trouble", in Jonathan Cott's, Bob *Dylan: The Essential Interviews*, 357.

19 Lewis Carroll, *Alice*, 29.

20 Jonathan Cott, *Bob Dylan: The Essential Interviews*, xi.

Alice: But aren't you Bob Dylan?

Bob smirks, surprised to be recognized by a young girl in the middle of the wood.

Bob: I'm only Bob Dylan when I have to be.[21]

Alice: But who are you the rest of the time?

Bob: Myself. [22]

Alice: Are you often more than one person?

Bob: Yes, I suppose I am.

Alice: That's quite all right. I often pretend to be two people as well. Sometimes many more.

Bob shoves his hand into his pocket and pulls out a pack of cigarettes, lights one, takes a quick drag, and exhales with a deep sigh. Alice watches with curiosity, then realizes her manners.

Alice: You may not have come for a cup of tea, but would you like one now that you're here?

Bob: Sure, I'll have a cup.

Bob pulls out the chair across from Alice's and sits down. Alice stands and busies herself with finding a tea pot that still has hot tea in it. The table is quite long, and she checks several pots before finding one to her satisfaction. Bob watches with curiosity as Alice brings two cups and saucers down from the far end of the table, fills them with steaming tea, and carefully places one before him. She sits

---

21 Jonathan Cott, Bob Dylan: *The Essential Interviews,* xi.

22 Ibid.

down with her own cup and takes a slow sip. He pauses a beat, waiting for her to speak. When she doesn't, he continues…

Bob: Do you like riddles?

Alice: I typically do, yes, but not in this place. She looks around and sighs. Here I find that riddles often have no answers.

Bob: Where are we?

Alice: I'm not really sure, to be honest.

Bob: I've fallen down quite the rabbit hole here, haven't I?

Alice's face brightens at the mention of the rabbit hole. She considers perhaps if this man has fallen down the same rabbit hole as she, then they may find their way out together.

Alice: You've fallen down the rabbit hole, too?

Bob: Oh, not a literal rabbit hole. You know, metaphorically speaking.

She looks a tad disheartened at the mention of metaphor. Not only because this means Bob likely cannot help her get home, but also because she cannot quite remember what the word metaphor means but is too embarrassed to say so.

Alice: That is just as well, as the falling does take quite a long time.

Bob takes a sip of his tea, which somehow tastes of both spiced apple and lemon custard tart. He removes the hat from his head, places the flowers from his hat into a vase on the table, and gives the hat a shake. As he shakes, the hat begins to relax and stretch into a long cream-colored scarf, which Bob wraps loosely around his neck.

Bob: What are you doing out here by yourself?

Alice: I've been having quite the adventure, but now I'm trying to find my way home.

Bob: How is that going?

Alice: Not well, I'm afraid. A man on a train once told me that I ought to know which way I'm going even if I don't know my own name. [23] Though I'm not certain I be lieve him. I'm not sure which is more important.

Bob: Your name, perhaps, is more important. You don't always need to know where you're going.

Alice: How is that?

Bob: If you don't know where you're going, any road will take you there.

Alice: The Cheshire cat gave me very similar advice.

Bob: I heard it from the Beatles.

Alice: I've also spoken to a beetle! He was also on the train. He wasn't very friendly though. Are the beetles friendlier where you come from?

Bob: They are. I generally have an excellent time with them. Apparently, I was the first person whoever got the Beatles high.

Alice: I grew to be quite high once...from eating a mushroom.

Bob: Yeah, they'll do that to you.

23 Lewis Carroll, *Through the Looking-Glass*, 151.

Alice finishes the last of her tea and pours herself and Bob another cup. As she reaches to across the table, she looks into Bob's eyes and some hint of familiarity rustles inside her.

Alice: I feel as though we've met before. Were you playing croquet earlier with the Duchess?

Bob: No, I was with Tweetledum and Tweetledee before I found you here. Quite an interested pair they are. Maybe I'll write a song about them someday.[24]

Alice: Yes, they are rather unusual. But here most things are. Perhaps we met in one of the Red King's dreams. The Tweetles seem to believe the King dreams others into existence quite often. Although I don't know that to be true.

Bob: How does someone go about finding their way into other people's dreams?

Alice: I should be more concerned about finding my way out.

Bob: I'll let you be in my dreams if I can be in yours.[25]

Alice: I don't want to belong to another person's dream. I don't want to be anyone's prisoner. I want to be a Queen. [26]

Bob: Queens are prisoners in their own right. Just because the queen owns the castle does not mean she is not also trapped inside it. Bob picks up a cloth napkin from the table and begins to wipe the white paint from his face. You need to find a way to be truly free.

---

24 Bob Dylan, "Love and Theft" (2001), track 1.
25 Bob Dylan, "Talkin' World War III Blues," track 10 from The Freewheelin' Bob Dylan, 1963.
26 Lewis Carroll, Through the Looking-Glass, 205-207.

Alice: And how does one get to be truly free?

Bob: To free one's mind, I suppose. To learn how to be your authentic self without guilt or insecurity. To realize that all I can do is be me—whoever that is. [27]

Bob stands and slings his bag over his shoulder.

Bob: Thank you for the tea.

Alice stands and curtsies.

Alice: Thank you for the company. One can get quite lonely here. She pauses a moment to straighten her dress and looks back into Bob's face. Have you thought of what you're looking for?

Bob: Answers, I suppose.

Alice: Have you found any?

Bob: Not a single one.

Alice: Perhaps the adventure is the most important part anyway.

Alice curtsies again and walks off into the wood. Bob turns to continue on the path from which he came. Once Bob reaches the path and enters into the wood himself, he realizes the sun had nearly set, as if he had stepped outside of time. Bob turns back to look for Alice, but both she and the table set for tea are gone.

27 Jonathan Cott, *Bob Dylan: The Essential Interviews*, 40.

Bibliography

Alexander, Michelle. "We Are Not the Resistance." New York Times, Sept. 21, 2018.

Carroll, Lewis. *Alice's Adventures in Wonderland and Through the Looking Glass*. New York: Signet Classics, 2000.

Cott, Jonathan. *Bob Dylan: The Essential Interviews*. New York: Wenner Books, 2007.

Dylan, Bob. *Chronicles, Volume One*. New York: Simon & Schuster, 2004.

Dylan, Bob. *The Nobel Lecture*. New York: Simon & Schuster, 2017.

Dylan, Bob, Joan Baez, Allen Ginsberg, Maria Muldaur, and Pete Seeger. 2005. *No Direction Home: Bob Dylan*. Hollywood, CA: Paramount Home Entertainment.

Haynes, Todd, dir. *I'm Not There*. 2007. Beverly Hills, CA: Endgame Entertainment.

Rolling Stone. "Bob Dylan: The Complete Album Guide." Rolling Stone, Special Collectors' Edition, 2017.

Thomas, Richard F. *Why Bob Dylan Matters*. New York: Harper Collins, 2017.

Discography

Beck. "Leopard-Skin Pill-Box Hat." (2009). Track 1 on *War Child – Heroes Vol. 1*. Parlophone UK, MP3.

Dylan, Bob. *Another Side of Bob Dylan*. (1964). Columbia Records, MP3.

Dylan, Bob. *Bob Dylan*. (1962). Columbia Records, MP3.

Dylan, Bob. *Bringing It All Back Home*. (1965). Columbia Records, MP3.

Dylan, Bob. *Highway 61 Revisited*. (1965). Columbia Records, MP3.

Dylan, Bob. "Like a Rolling Stone." (1965). Track 1 on *Highway 61 Revisited*. Columbia Records, MP3.

Dylan, Bob. *Slow Train Coming*. (1979). Columbia Records, MP3.

Dylan, Bob. *The Freewheelin' Bob Dylan*. (1963). Columbia Records, MP3.

Dylan, Bob. *The Times They Are A-Changin'*. (1964). Columbia Records, MP3.

Dylan, Bob, "You're Gonna Make Me Lonesome When You Go." (1975). Track 5 on *Blood on the Tracks*. Columbia Records, MP3.

First Aid Kit. "It Ain't Me Babe." YouTube Video. 3:55, October 16, 2016. https://www.youtube.com/watch?v=pyPly62Ad9M

Jarosz, Sarah. "Ring Them Bells." Released May 17, 2011. Track 4 on *Follow Me Down*. Sugar Hill Records, MP3.

Marling, Laura. "A Hard Rain's A-Gonna Fall." Recorded 2017. More Alarming Records, MP3.

Matthews, Dave (Band). "All Along the Watchtower." The Gorge, George, WA, Sept. 20, 2011.

Matthews, Dave (Band). "All Along the Watchtower." Central Park, New York, NY, Jan. 3, 2019.

Lumineers. "Subterranean Homesick Blues." Rocket Mortgage Field House, Cleveland, OH, Feb. 8, 2020.

Acknowledgements

I'd like to start by once again thanking Rob Jackson for believing that two poems feverishly recited in the late night hours after too much whiskey were deserving of a full-length manuscript. I would have never written this book without you.

Thank you to Red Giant Books for believing in Rob believing in me. You've made a dream of mine come true. For that, I am eternally grateful.

Thank you to Sara Dobie Bauer for declaring that I could write a book, for telling me that more than once, and for being so gracious and generous with your expertise and encouragement.

To Wes McMasters, for your thoughtful insight and feedback. You are one of my favorite poets and all those Friday night open-mics so long ago are some of my favorite memories.

Lastly, thank you to my husband, Mitch, for being my sounding board, my first reader, and the greatest support. You've given your critical eye, time, and attention to this project and I wouldn't have finished it without you.

www.ingramcontent.com/pod-product-compliance
Lightning Source LLC
LaVergne TN
LVHW041229080426
835508LV00011B/1127

9781732551473